CW01455666

BILD Code of Practice
for minimising the use of restrictive physical interventions: planning, developing and delivering training

A guide for purchasers of training, training organisations and trainers

Fourth edition

British Library Cataloguing in Publication Data

A CIP record for this book is available from the Public Library

© BILD Publications 2001, 2006, 2010

Fourth edition 2014

BILD Publications is the imprint of:

British Institute of Learning Disabilities
Birmingham Research Park
97 Vincent Drive
Edgbaston
Birmingham B15 2SQ

Telephone: 0121 415 6960

E-mail: enquiries@bild.org.uk

Website: www.bild.org.uk

ISBN 978 1 905218 33 2

BILD Publications are distributed by:

BookSource
50 Cambuslang Road
Cambuslang
Glasgow G32 8NB

Telephone: 0845 370 0067

Fax: 0845 370 0068

For a publications catalogue with details of all BILD books and journals e-mail enquiries@bild.org.uk or visit the BILD website www.bild.org.uk

Printed in the UK by Latimer Trend and Company Ltd, Plymouth

People with learning disabilities and people with autism want to make their own choices and decisions about the things that affect their lives. To help make this happen, BILD works to influence policy-makers and campaigns for change, and our services can help organisations improve their service design and develop their staff to deliver great support.

Contents

Acknowledgements

BILD thanks the many individuals and organisations that continue to contribute to its work in the field of positive behaviour support and minimising the use of restrictive practices. In particular BILD thanks all those who support its work in relation to the Accreditation Scheme. We welcome the continued and enthusiastic support for an external assessment process from education, health and social care organisations. The Accreditation Scheme panel members and assessors are an integral and invaluable part of this work and their professionalism and commitment is acknowledged here.

In developing this fourth edition of the *Code of Practice*, BILD is grateful to all of the individuals and organisations, including those from the accredited organisations, who responded to the consultation and to those representatives of other organisations who attended focus groups and consultation workshops to further contribute to the development of this *Code of Practice* and the Accreditation Scheme. In particular, BILD is grateful to Phil Howell, who helped prepare this fourth edition and the following individuals who agreed to act as critical readers of the draft fourth edition – David Allen, Martin Bertulis, Glyn Connolly, Bill Fox, Alan Jefferson, Alan Martin and Chris Stirling.

Introduction

This is the fourth edition of the *BILD Code of Practice*. The first edition was published in 2001 (BILD, 2001). It follows on from the second and third editions that were published in 2006 and 2010 respectively (BILD, 2006 and 2010).

The frequency with which the *Code of Practice* has required updating says something about the advances in thinking and the pace of change in the development of good practice in reducing restrictive practices in education and care settings for individuals whose behaviour is described as challenging services. However, running along-side the positive developments have been a series of national scandals exposing abuse and poor care practices, most notably the Panorama programme about abuse at the Winterbourne View Hospital (BBC, 2011). One outcome of the documentary and the national outcry that followed its broadcast has been an increased government focus, in England, on the models of care, inspec-tion and regulation systems, standards of practice and guidance underpinning the provision of care to adults and children with learning disabilities, autism and special educational needs (Depart-ment of Health, 2012a, 2012b). The impetus for this new edition is, therefore, twofold. First, it incorporates the most up to date thinking within the field, notably the increasing prominence of positive behaviour support approaches. Second, it takes account of the new guidance *Positive and Proactive Care: Reducing the need for restrictive interventions* (Department of Health, 2014) in England that aims to minimise the use of restrictive practices, promote safer application of restrictive practices as a last resort and alternatives in the management of challenging behaviour in health and adult social care.

Background

The initial *Code of Practice* (BILD, 2001) was aimed at trainers and was a response to an identified need to clarify the standards relating to training in physical intervention skills. This first edition of the *Code of Practice* was written at the same time as the Department of Health and the Department for Education and Skills were preparing the *Guidance for Restrictive Physical Interventions: How to provide safe services for people with learning disabilities and autistic spectrum disorder* (Department of Health and Department for Education and Skills, 2002). BILD worked closely with the two government departments during the drafting of the guidance and this ensured that there were many common themes in the *Code of Practice*. In 2001, the focus of the first edition of the *Code of Practice* was to address the need to ensure that physical interventions were used safely and within the law.

The first edition set out clear principles including:

- Training in physical interventions must always be provided within a wider context that promotes prevention and alternative ways of responding to challenging behaviour.

- Physical interventions must be planned with reference to the individual's support plan that is produced following multidisciplinary assessments. Blanket approaches that permit the routine use of physical interventions in an education or care setting are unacceptable.

- Only physical intervention techniques that have been assessed as safe and are not based on inflicting pain should be used.

- Physical interventions must only be used in a person's best interests and in the context of an organisation's duty of care to the people it looks after.

- To comply with the law, physical interventions can only be considered as a last resort and must be the least restrictive alternative that will manage the behaviour.

- If a physical intervention is used, it must be at the minimum practicable level to manage the behaviour and be used for the shortest possible time.

All of these principles remain as relevant today as they were in 2001.

The 2006 edition of the *Code of Practice* extended its target readership to include the commissioners, or purchasers, of training as well as trainers. This was an acknowledgement that good quality training, on its own, is insufficient to ensure good support. The revised *Code of Practice* recognised the importance of physical interventions being used within an overall framework of good practice and that a wide range of preventative measures should be put in place to ensure that they are only used as a last resort. This preventative framework requires care and education organisations to have clear and robust policies that are based on a care planning approach. This will include a gradient of preventative measures to diffuse challenging situations before there is any need to resort to physical interventions. In addition organisations need effective monitoring systems to ensure that members of staff only use physical interventions in this wider preventative context. The 2006 *Code of Practice* aimed to assist commissioners of training to better understand the links between the training and their organisational context, helping them to make better decisions about what training to arrange or purchase. This edition of the *Code of Practice* took account of the guidance in England that had been published since 2001 (Department of Health and Department for Education and Skills, 2002). For training organisations and trainers, it also took account of the development of BILD's Physical Interventions Accreditation Scheme that had been launched in April 2002. Accreditation is conditional on training organisations ensuring that the training they offer meets with the requirements of the *Code of Practice*.

The 2010 edition of the *Code of Practice* included a much greater emphasis on:

- the importance of positive behaviour support approaches

- the importance of reducing the use of restrictive physical interventions

- issues relating to poor practice as the publication coincided with a number of widely publicised abuse scandals in Cornwall and Sutton and Merton (Healthcare Commission and Commission for Social Care Inspection, 2006 and Healthcare Commission, 2007)

- examples of good practice and the ways in which vulnerable children, young people and adults could be positively supported

- the importance of appropriate cultures within care and education services

The 2010 *Code of Practice* represented a progressive movement from an approach that emphasised making training in physical skills better to an approach that emphasised restraint reduction. It included a greater emphasis on training organisations and commissioners of training providing evidence that restraint reduction plans were being developed and implemented. There was a stronger emphasis on ensuring that training took account of the education, health or social care organisation's values and culture, the context in which the training was being delivered and the assessed needs of the individuals using that service.

Continuous improvements

In publishing this fourth edition of the *Code of Practice*, BILD remains fully committed to providing standards for the key individuals and organisations involved in the development and delivery of restraint reduction training that includes training in physical skills. BILD continues to be morally and ethically opposed to the deliberate infliction of pain as a means of control in the care and education of the children, young people and adults covered by this guidance. This updated edition of the *Code of Practice* continues to have application across a variety of settings. It is relevant to education, health and social care organisations that purchase training on minimising the use of restrictive practices including the use of physical skills, for the following:

- children and adults with a learning disability

- children and adults with autistic spectrum conditions

- pupils with special educational needs

- children with additional needs that may result in socially inappropriate behaviour(s)

- children with social and emotional difficulties associated with behaviours that challenge

- adults with a learning disability and/or autism who are detained under the mental health legislation for the country in which they live

- children and young people (up to the age of 19) who are detained in semi secure and secure settings or who are detained under the relevant mental health legislation

- families and family carers, including foster carers, those offering short breaks and support to children, young people and adults with learning disabilities, autism and social emotional and behaviour difficulties

This edition has been published in a national policy context (in England) where there appears to be little or no enthusiasm for the mandatory regulation of training providers. Instead, quality services are promoted through guidance and good practice guides. In the absence of mandatory regulation, the BILD Accreditation Scheme based on this *Code of*

Practice, will remain one of the few available mechanisms to enable training providers to have a focussed external verification of the quality of their service. A growing number of training organisations are applying for accreditation and for these, and the existing accredited organisations, this *Code of Practice* will continue to be a set of standards against which their services can be benchmarked and assessed. For more information on the BILD Accreditation Scheme go to www.bild.org.uk/codeofpractice

However, the use of physical interventions is just one component of the wider training and development frameworks that support children, young people and adults who can experience difficulties in communication or managing their emotions and use behaviours as a means to express themselves. This revised and updated *Code of Practice* will continue to provide an important point of reference not just for trainers but also for training organisations, for the purchasers of training, for those with responsibility for implementing standards and for the family members and advocates of individuals who have challenging behaviours. Information about this *Code of Practice* for regulators, family members, advocates and individuals who use services can be found at www.bild.org.uk/codeofpractice

In addition to continuing to provide a framework for the BILD Accreditation Scheme, the *Code of Practice* also:

- helps training and purchasing organisations to shape the content of bespoke training and create a focus on the essential values, knowledge and skills in relation to risk assessment, prevention and minimising the use of restrictive practices

- supports purchasing organisations to identify the risks associated with challenging behaviour in their services and how to manage those risks appropriately by using available resources in the most appropriate way

- supports purchasing organisations to develop high quality preventative and proactive strategies that include policy development, reporting and recording systems, as well as support arrangements for individuals who use their service, family members and the staff who support them

- balances the rights and responsibilities of individuals who use their service and staff members in a framework that acknowledges that their joint safety, dignity and wellbeing is of critical importance

- increases awareness of current relevant legislation, policies and guidance

- supports training and purchasing organisations to agree on the structure, content, frequency and duration of training

- supports the development of individual trainers

- provides a resource within which high quality training in behaviour support and physical skills can be promoted and delivered.

Training and purchasing organisations that fully adopt the principles of the *Code of Practice* are able to:

- demonstrate that they have an appropriate support framework that is underpinned by robust quality policies

- provide evidence that the training, care and education offered reflects the individual needs of the children, young people and adults they support

- demonstrate that they have appropriate assessment processes in place

- demonstrate that they adopt a proactive and non-aversive approach to supporting individuals

- demonstrate a commitment to taking account of and reducing risk in services

- provide evidence of a staff group that has received appropriate training and supervision to enable them to offer care and support, learning opportunities and skill acquisition in a safe environment that is free from abusive practices

- demonstrate a reduced reliance on aversive practices and the use of physical interventions and a commitment to further developing restraint reduction plans

Most important of all, it is hoped that the *Code of Practice* will contribute to improvements in the quality of life and support experienced by the children, young people and adults who come into contact with services.

Structure and layout of the
Code of Practice

The structure of this fourth edition of the *Code of Practice* is different to that of the earlier editions. It recognises the key contributions of the education, health and social care organisations that purchase training (purchasing organisations), of the organisations that provide training (training organisations) and of the individual trainers themselves by structuring the material in three sections, one for each key stakeholder group. Apart from where statutory responsibilities are referred to for purchasing organisations, the

Code of Practice represents good practice advice – things that they 'should' do or are 'recommended' or 'urged' to do if they want to be able to demonstrate and provide evidence of good practice as BILD has no authority to require their adherence to the *Code of Practice*. Accredited training organisations, those aspiring to accreditation and individual trainers have a much greater imperative to comply with the *Code of Practice's* requirements since BILD accreditation is conditional on compliance. For these groups, there is a much greater emphasis on things that 'must' be done.

BILD has provided additional information in suitable formats for regulators and health and social care commissioners, people with a learning disability and/or autistic spectrum conditions, family members and advocates on our website at www.bild.org.uk/codeofpractice to enable them to become familiar with the contents of the new *Code of Practice*.

BILD firmly believes that whole organisation approaches to supporting individuals whose behaviour is described as challenging offers the greatest likelihood of good outcomes for them. This belief is supported by a growing evidence base. We demonstrate this belief by our continuing and sustained commitment to positive behaviour support as an approach to minimise the use of all types of restrictive practices. A whole organisational approach emphasises the crucial impact on quality of embedding good practice in the day to day support offered by education, health or social care services. Robust and rigorous training is only one element of positive behaviour support and minimising the use of restrictive practices, but it provides an important opportunity to:

- set out clearly the rights and values that underpin good education and care alongside the theoretical principles of positive behaviour support and restraint reduction planning

- ensure that there are clear and robust organisational and individual decision making systems in place to make sure that the day to day lives of individuals are underpinned by informed decisions about appropriate interventions

- assist organisations to evaluate the extent to which they are 'fit for purpose' and have in place rigorous policies, procedures and governance

- provide consistency in support across organisational boundaries by developing common approaches; this is particularly important for individuals whose day to day education and care needs are met by a range of separate organisations and professionals

The fundamental purpose of this fourth edition of the *Code of Practice* is to help bring consistency to the development and delivery of training courses and to the governance, policies and procedures of the organisations where the training courses are delivered. The *Code of Practice* and the BILD Accreditation Scheme should not, however, be the only measures by which purchasing organisations, training organisations and trainers should assure themselves of quality. The *Code of Practice* is able to signpost people to many other sources of guidance, including those that are statutory. This edition of the *Code of Practice* is a key resource for all those who wish to minimise the use of restrictive practices as part of a positive behaviour support programme that aims to improve the quality of life for individuals using services.

Alan Jefferson
Chair of BILD Trustees and Chair of the BILD Accreditation Scheme

Purchasing organisations

Purchasers of training (purchasing organisations) have a responsibility to ensure that their operational practices and the training they commission provides the best possible life experiences for the individuals they educate or support. In order to do this they should take account of the following:

1.1 Providing a framework for positive behaviour support and minimising the use of restrictive practices

1.1.1   Purchasing organisations have a responsibility to ensure that the culture, values, attitudes, knowledge and skills base within their organisation embrace the principles and practices of positive behaviour support including:

- a commitment to promote positive behaviour support and primary prevention based upon comprehensive functional assessment, as the preferred approach to behavioural intervention

- recognising that using physical interventions is a restrictive practice and that their use should always be as a last resort when all other alternatives have been considered and found to be either ineffective or inappropriate

- using a gradient and gradual approach to the use of necessary force within a framework that takes account of the level of risk to the individual and others

- ensuring the use of restrictive physical interventions only occurs when this is in the agreed best interest of the individual concerned and is accompanied by a rigorous individual risk assessment

1.1.2   The above principles and practices should be reflected in the organisation's written values, mission statement and policies.

1.1.3   Information about incidents of behaviour that challenge and the use of any restrictive physical intervention should be routinely collected by the organisation, evaluated and the lessons learnt should be used to improve daily practice.

1.1.4   Through their written statements on approaches to behaviour that challenges, purchasing organisations should show an understanding that implementing positive behaviour support across whole services is an important way of reducing reliance on restrictive approaches and the use of restrictive physical interventions.

1.1.5   Individuals who use a service, family members and advocates should be able to obtain information from a purchasing organisation about the aims and values of the organisation and its policies and procedures including those on positive behaviour support and the use of restrictive practices. This information should be in a format that best suits their communication requirements and needs. This information should explain how the purchasing organisation:

- protects and upholds the human rights of individuals who use the service

- works to enhance the quality of life of the individuals using the service through the provision of person centred support

- makes sure that there are opportunities for each individual to participate in the planning and delivery of their support and that they are involved in decisions about their care or education

- makes sure that people are treated with compassion, dignity and kindness

- makes sure that individuals are kept safe and free from harm

- makes sure that individuals have the opportunity to maintain and develop positive relationships

1.1.6   Purchasing organisations should ensure that any programme of learning covering reactive management and restrictive physical intervention skills is taught within a broader framework of positive behaviour support. The rationale for the inclusion of any physical skills, including breakaway techniques, in a training model or programme of learning should be agreed at the most senior management level.

1.1.7   Purchasing organisations should ensure that the culture within their organisation promotes primary prevention and a commitment to reducing the use of restrictive physical interventions. Allen (2011) identified eight characteristics of successful restraint reduction initiatives. BILD recommends that purchasing organisations conduct regular self appraisal against the characteristics described in this publication.

1.1.8   Purchasing organisations have a responsibility to undertake a training needs analysis. This should be underpinned by a behavioural audit and risk assessment that identifies the challenges that the training is required to address. This should be completed for the whole service.

1.1.9   Behavioural audits should include information on behaviour types. This should identify the frequency, duration and severity, where the incidents are taking place and those likely to be affected by such incidents. They should also detail the extent of the current use of restrictive physical interventions in numbers and as a percentage of responses to all incidents of behaviour that challenges.

1.1.10   The risk assessment should describe the level of assessed risk over the past six months within the services identified to receive the training.

1.1.11   The training needs analysis should examine the effectiveness of current policy statements, behaviour support plans and staff support mechanisms.

1.1.12   Purchasing organisations should provide a written summary of criteria 1.1.9, 1.1.10 and 1.1.11 to the training organisation to inform the curriculum development. This will contribute to the rationale for the selection and teaching of specific, personal safety, breakaway and restrictive physical interventions.

1.1.13   Purchasing organisations should provide a written summary of the current use of other forms of restrictive practices to inform the development of any training curriculum.

1.1.14   Organisations that deliver their training using in-house trainers must ensure that all training is undertaken based on a current behaviour audit. Behaviour audits must be conducted prior to the delivery of each training course and should be undertaken with reference to the participants' place of employment.

1.1.15   Training should take account of the purchasing organisation's culture and ways of working including its philosophy, mission statement, policies, approach to managing challenging behaviour and its staffing levels.

1.1.16   Purchasing organisations should ensure that the training organisation only employs trainers who are suitably qualified, skilled and experienced to competently deliver the commissioned training and manage each participant's learning and develop-ment needs during course delivery (see sections 2 and 3 of the *Code of Practice*).

1.2   Organisational policies and procedures

1.2.1   Prior to the commencement of training, purchasers need to ensure that they have developed and implemented an appropriate policy framework that includes:

- a clear statement of the values of the organisation

- references to the principles of positive behaviour support and person centred approaches
- an overview of the legislative framework that relates to the organisation and to its use of restrictive practices
- an overview of the current relevant national guidance
- information about good practice resources
- information about the rights of individuals who use the services, family members and advocates and how they are involved in the care provided at an individual, operational and strategic level
- a complaints process that is accessible to the individuals who use the service, family members, advocates and any significant others
- the procedures and documentation for any planned behavioural interventions including primary, secondary and reactive strategies
- confirmation of the organisation's commitment to the principles of least restrictive alternatives, gradient responses and reasonable force
- a commitment to post incident management, debriefing and support systems for individuals who use the service and staff
- information about how the organisation reports, records and reviews incidents
- information about the roles and responsibilities of all those involved in the organisation's behaviour support framework

1.2.2   Purchasing organisations should provide a copy of their current policies to the training organisation so that they can be referenced in the training content.

1.2.3   Purchasing organisations need to demonstrate that all individuals who use their services have behaviour support plans, which include primary and secondary strategies and aim to prevent and/or reduce the use of restrictive practices. Behaviour support plans must be developed in partnership with the individuals concerned and the people who know the individual best, this may be their family members, friends and advocate.

1.2.4   Behaviour support plans must include the specific details of individualised reactive management strategies including any required restrictive practices. These must take account of the individual's unique circumstances. Behaviour support plans should include broader consideration of the support and training needs of the individual's wider circle of support including the needs of family members, friends and their advocate.

1.2.5   All individuals being supported by the purchasing organisation should have access to any information about their behaviour assessment, support plan or intervention strategy. This should be in a format that suits their communication requirements and needs.

1.2.6   Purchasers should ensure that whenever a planned physical intervention response is developed to support an individual, a reduction plan is also included to ensure that positive behaviour support strategies can replace a restrictive physical interventions response, as soon as possible. The plan should include an individual behaviour risk assessment. This risk assessment should document:

- an assessment of the individual's behaviour, its impact and who is affected

- an assessment of the individual's physiological and psychological wellbeing

- a review of the above two points that demonstrates that any restrictive physical interventions used as a reactive approach do not unnecessarily or unreasonably present a greater risk of harm to the individual than the identified behaviour

- any underlying conditions that may prohibit the use of specific physical interventions

It is likely that such information will be maintained as part of the behaviour support plans or the positive handling plans.

1.2.7   Purchasing organisations must comply with national and local safeguarding policies, procedures and guidance. Reference must be made to the advice and guidance offered by the Independent Safeguarding Authority (or the relevant authority for the country that the purchasing organisation is operating in) and to the current safeguarding legislation and guidance for either children's or adult services for that country. Further information about this and other key legislation and guidance relating to the four UK nations can be found at www.bild.org.uk/codeofpractice

1.2.8   Purchasing organisations need to provide clear information to their employees on how to raise concerns relating to abuse and poor practice. There should be a thorough induction programme where employees receive training on abuse and safeguarding and about whistle-blowing policies and procedures. Information about how to report poor practice should include references to reporting the misuse and abuse of restrictive physical interventions arising from:

- the inappropriate and excessive use of force or any form of restraint (physical, environmental, chemical, mechanical, or psychological)

- inflicting pain and/or injury

- the use of threats, punishment or intimidation

- unauthorised deprivations or restrictions of liberty

- failure to implement an agreed behaviour support plan

- trainers abusing their position by providing information and/or advice that does not reflect the values of a positive behaviour support approach

1.2.9 As part of their statutory safeguarding processes purchasing organisations must demonstrate a clear procedure for responding to disclosures of abuse and poor practice. Purchasing organisations must share this procedure with any training organisation that they purchase services from so that the procedure can be followed should disclosures or whistleblowing arise during training.

1.2.10 Purchasing organisations should provide appropriate support to their staff through team meetings, staff supervision, incident reviews and service reviews that include the ongoing monitoring of the use of restrictive physical interventions. The lead manager allocated to receive review information must have relevant knowledge, skills and experience that enables them to meet their responsibilities effectively.

1.3   Best interests

1.3.1   Purchasing organisations should provide their employees with training that is evidence based and that equips each member of staff with the knowledge and skills appropriate to their day to day practice. Purchasing organisations should ensure that the training positively influences staff attitudes, develops practical skills in supporting behaviours that challenge, provides supports for behaviour change and increases the quality of life of the individuals that they support.

1.3.2   Behavioural risk assessment is important in reducing risk, improving longer term planning and supporting individuals who present services with challenging behaviour. In addition, it enables the development of training that will increase the skills required to reduce the identified risks. Purchasing organisations should ensure that they have appropriate behaviour risk assessment procedures in place.

1.3.3   Training should offer the required knowledge and skills to increase every participant's ability to engage in reflective practice so that they are able to work better with behaviours that are described as challenging.

1.3.4   Purchasing organisations have a duty to determine and record the decision making process when it is judged to be in the best interests of an individual to include restrictive physical interventions in their behaviour support plan. The organisation's policies and procedures for determining and recording best interest decisions should take account of the relevant capacity legislation for the country they work in.

1.3.5   All individuals are assumed to have capacity, unless a specific assessment identifies that they lack the capacity to make a specific decision. If this happens, a documented 'best interest' decision must be made using the best interest decision making guidance as set out in relevant capacity legislation. For further details see www.bild.org.uk/codeofpractice

1.3.6   Best interest decisions on the use of restrictive physical interventions should reflect both the principles of the relevant legislation and this *Code of Practice*. Therefore the use of restrictive physical interventions must:

- only be considered when all other available and appropriate methods of primary and secondary prevention and non-physical reactive intervention have been tried, reviewed, evaluated and judged to be ineffective

- be a last resort for dealing with specific behaviour that challenges and the risks presented

---

- employ the minimum reasonable amount of force

- be used for the shortest possible time

- be followed by a debrief for all of those involved, which is appropriate to their needs and individual requirements. If a restrictive physical intervention was used as an emergency or unplanned response, consideration should be given to under-taking a full behaviour assessment of the individual and developing a new or revised support plan

- be determined by a behaviour assess-ment and support plan and include a restrictive physical intervention reduction plan. The plan should be reviewed following any incident that results in the use of a restrictive physical intervention. All of the plans should be subject to review on a regular basis and at least every six months

1.3.7 For adult health and social care services in England decision making must take account of Section 58 of the Department of Health guidance *Positive and Proactive Care: Reducing the need for restrictive interventions.* This will mean that for any form of restrictive practice to be deemed an appropriate intervention, and in the best interests of the individual the following must be addressed:

- Restrictive interventions should never be used to punish or for the sole intention of inflicting pain, suffering or humiliation.

- There must be a real possibility of harm to the person or to staff, the public or others if no action is undertaken.

- The nature of techniques used to restrict must be proportionate to the risk of harm and the seriousness of that harm.

- Any action taken to restrict a person's freedom of movement must be the least restrictive option that will meet the need.

- Any restriction should be imposed for no longer than absolutely necessary.

- What is done to people, why and with what consequences must be subject to audit and monitoring and must be open and transparent.

- Restrictive interventions should only ever be used as a last resort.

- People who use services, carers and advocate involvement is essential when reviewing plans for restrictive interventions.

(Department of Health, 2014)

1.3.8 Purchasing organisations should have appropriate policies in place that ensure the views of the individuals who use the service

---

and family members are fully included in strategic and operational decision making, in the quality checking of the organisation and in the development of an individual's support plans. Individuals and their family members should also be involved in planning, developing and delivering training and reviewing organisational policies and procedures.

1.4   Risk assessment and health and safety

1.4.1   Organisations purchasing training have a responsibility for the occupational health of their employees. Written information regarding the physical requirements for course participants should be provided, by the training organisation, prior to course attendance. This should be used by managers to determine whether or not a participant is fit to attend and participate. Where there are concerns about a participant's ability to attend and participate in any training, an independent occupational assessment should be undertaken so that additional advice and guidance can be sought. In situations when an occupational assessment suggests that an employee cannot attend training, it is the purchasing organisation's responsibility to consider the wider implication of this assessment with regard to the individual's ability to work in their current setting.

1.4.2   Purchasing organisations should provide advice on the appropriate clothing and footwear to be worn during training. They should confirm that trainers reserve the right to exclude any individual who they consider to be dressed inappropriately for the training or who during the training acts in a manner that may compromise their safety or that of others.

1.4.3   Purchasing organisations should confirm to the trainer that they are satisfied that all participants are fit to be at work and therefore to participate in the training. Each course participant should sign a health declaration and return this to their line manager or training department prior to attending the training.

1.4.4   Purchasing organisations and participants share the responsibility for their health and safety in relation to both attendance (including the suitability and appropriateness of the training; the training venue; and the physical activities undertaken during the training) and their ongoing fitness to practice the restrictive physical interventions in the workplace.

1.4.5   Purchasing organisations whose own employees deliver training in-house, on their behalf and under licence, from an accredited provider must ensure that first aid support is available when training is taking place on site. Good practice is for first aid equipment to be available in the training room and at least one trainer should possess an up to date first aid qualification.

1.4.6   Organisations that deliver services and employ in-house trainers or that run training on their own premises should ensure that their insurance specifically covers this activity.

1.4.7   Restrictive physical interventions taught to staff should be appropriate to the needs of the individuals they support or educate and the assessed level of risk and their workplace. Training in restrictive physical interventions should prepare staff to manage the assessed risks that are typically found in the service in which they are employed and should not focus on possible extremes of behaviour that are unlikely to happen.

1.4.8   Following training, purchasing organisations should be able to demonstrate an appropriate procedure to identify and address any competence issues in the use of restrictive physical interventions. This may lead to decisions about whether employees are at risk in specific work settings if they are not deemed competent to use a required restrictive physical intervention.

1.5   Course curriculum development

1.5.1   Purchasing organisations need to be able to clearly articulate the outcomes they wish to achieve by purchasing training. These outcomes should be shared with the training organisation so that they can inform the learning aims and objectives.

1.5.2   Purchasing organisations should develop a clear procedure to assess the achievement of these outcomes following training delivery and their impact on daily practice.

1.5.3   There is an expectation that the staff and managers at all levels in the purchasing organisation are aware of the training that is delivered in their services. Those with corporate responsibility for service delivery should agree to the content of the curriculum, including the training of specific physical skills. In adult services this will include the senior leadership team or executive board. In schools, colleges and pupil referral units this will include head teachers, the board of governors and the management committee.

1.5.4   Purchasing organisations that agree a curriculum that includes physical skills with a trainer should:

- provide a written statement of context and rationale, supported by a behavioural audit, risk assessment and training needs analysis

---

- agree and sign off the physical skills to be taught at board or senior management level, recognising that different physical skills may be required in different services within the same organisation

- be aware of the psychological and physio-logical risk assessments of the specific techniques agreed with the training organisation

1.5.5   Purchasing organisations should ensure that all participants attending training are informed that there will be a formal test of what they have learnt, as part of the course. Specific details of how this will be done (eg written, multiple choice) must be provided so that any special requirements for participants can be accommodated during the training.

1.5.6   Purchasing organisations should set out a clear process for supporting any participant who fails or is referred by the training organisation. This process should set out the development of an individual action plan to provide additional support to the participant and to assign responsibility for each action. This should also include discussion of any individual learning requirements that may need to be supported and addressed.

1.6 Continuous review of the quality, effectiveness and relevance of training

1.6.1   BILD expects that training in physical skills will be refreshed annually (within 12 months of initial training) in all settings. However, purchasing organisations should be mindful of the Health and Safety at Work Act 1974 and their responsibility to ensure the continuing competence of their employees. Therefore, they should provide training as regularly as is necessary to ensure that such competence is maintained.

1.6.2   Refresher training should address the theoretical and practical curriculum needs of the participants. This does not mean simply repeating the previous training, rather it should be an exploration of how the concepts, theories and approaches previously learnt have been used and developed in the intervening period. Refresher training should explore how these are being applied or not applied as well as providing any update on new guidance and legislation and specific physical skills if necessary.

1.6.3   Purchasing organisations have a duty under health and safety legislation to ensure that practicable steps are taken to continually ensure the safety of their employees. Formal refresher training may be one of the steps taken. Purchasing organisations should work in partnership with their training organisation and organisational decision makers, such as their executive boards for trusts, school governors, local education authorities and senior managers, to ensure the provision of refresher courses that maintain staff skills at a level that is appropriate to their working environment.

1.6.4   There is limited evidence stating how effective training remains over time and over what time period staff are able to accurately retain physical skills and apply them as intended. Taking into account the limited evidence and the duty of employers as stated above, BILD recommends that staff should attend formal refresher training, every 12 months, as a minimum. The purpose of refresher training should be to review practice in the participant's work setting, including revisiting and refreshing their knowledge of proactive support and de-escalation. In addition participants will need to refresh their knowledge of the safe and appropriate application of any physical skills that they have been taught, if they are still required in their work setting.

1.6.5   Purchasing organisations should review the appropriateness and effectiveness of the training and course content taught within the service annually.

1.6.6	Purchasing organisations should ensure that appropriate support and debriefing is available to all of their employees who may be required to support people who exhibit behaviour that challenges.
1.6.7	Purchasing organisations should be mindful of their obligations to their employees and their duty to comply with health and safety legislation.
1.6.8	Purchasing organisations are reminded of the need to balance the rights of the individuals who use their service with those of the people employed to support or educate them.
1.6.9	At least annually, purchasing organisations should establish a process for reviewing critical incidents and ensuring that any lessons learnt are included in organisational planning and to inform workforce development and training. There must be clear guidelines on where the information about critical incidents goes, who collates it, how it is used and how feedback is provided to those involved and to the organisation as a whole.
1.6.10	At least annually, purchasing organisations should formally review corporate data on the rates of behaviours that challenge and on the rates of use of restrictive physical interventions. This data should be supported by up to date risk assessments.

1.6.11   Purchasing organisations should formally review all information relating to injuries or dangerous occurrences associated with the use of restrictive physical interventions, both during training and in application in the workplace. This review should take place on a regular basis and at least annually and appropriate action should be taken if any concerns or failings are identified.

Training organisations

Training organisations have a responsibility to ensure that the training they develop and deliver takes account of the following:

2.1 Training within a framework of positive behaviour support

2.1.1 Training organisations delivering courses in minimising the use of restrictive practices and physical interventions must ensure that the training delivered is within a context that promotes the importance of positively supporting individuals and of preventing behaviour which may present a challenge to services. This should be balanced with information about the rights of employees and the obligations of employers under the relevant legislation and guidance.

2.1.2 Training organisations and purchasing organisations must consider ways to reduce

---

the use of restrictive practices, as part of the training needs analysis, and provide alternative positive strategies for preventing and managing challenging behaviour. The outcomes of this consideration should be taken into account in the training curriculum.

2.1.3   During initial discussions with the purchasing organisation, the responsibility for undertaking the training needs analysis that includes risk assessments and behaviour audits should be agreed and recorded.

2.1.4   Training organisations must ensure that they and their employees promote the principle that restrictive physical interventions should only be considered when all other reasonable alternatives have been considered and found to be ineffective or inappropriate. The training they provide should take account of the level of risk presented by individuals in specific services and documented in the training needs analysis.

2.1.5   Throughout the taught curriculum, an appropriate emphasis must be placed on the ongoing assessment of behaviour with an overall aim of improving the quality of life for the individual. This should include the functional aspects of behaviour and the primary and secondary strategies for the prevention of behaviour that challenges.

2.1.6   In order to support the continuity and consistency of approaches across service boundaries any individual, member of an individual's family or advocate should be able to obtain information on the training content delivered to a paid member of staff supporting the individual. This should be in a format that they can understand.

2.2 Training that supports local and national policy

2.2.1   Training organisations must only provide training to organisations that have a current written policy that relates to the support of people whose behaviours challenge. The policy needs to contain statements on the use of restrictive physical interventions including:

- a clear statement of the values of the organisation

- the organisation's approach to proactive support and the prevention of challenging behaviour

- the rights of the individuals who use the service, their family members and/or advocates

- reactive strategies for managing behaviour that challenges

- the organisation's commitment to a gradient approach that addresses the principle of least restrictive physical intervention and the principle of minimum force

- the available debriefing and staff support systems

- the legislative framework within which restrictive interventions are used

- national and local guidance and policy (see criteria 2.2.3)

- a commitment to the principles described within this *Code of Practice*

2.2.2   Where there is no policy, the training organisation should support the purchasing organisation to develop and implement an appropriate policy as soon as is practicably possible and prior to any training being delivered.

2.2.3   Training must make reference to and place emphasis on the current national policy and guidance for the country the training is being delivered in. The training organisation must be consistent with the relevant legislation and good practice guidance for the jurisdiction in which the purchasing organisation or specific service operates. Up to date information on the relevant legislation, policies and guidance for England, Northern Ireland, Scotland and Wales can be found on the BILD website at www.bild.org.uk/codeofpractice

2.2.4   Training must directly address and incorporate all relevant local policies, including those on behaviour support, restrictive practices, safeguarding of children and/or adults, whistleblowing, capacity, deprivation of liberty and communication. This list is not exhaustive.

2.2.5   Training organisations should ensure that the national legislation and guidance referred to in the training is relevant to the sector and the needs of the individuals that the participants are supporting. Training organisations have a duty to ensure that they regularly review and update their training content in light of any new guidance being published. Training organisations can consult the Accreditation Scheme pages of the BILD website at www.bild.org.uk/codeofpractice for information on any new legislation and guidance relating to the sectors and countries covered by this *Code of Practice*.

2.3   Training to implement best interest criteria

2.3.1   Training content should include information on best interest decision making that is presented within the principles of this *Code of Practice*, the purchaser's organisational policy and national legislation and guidance.

2.3.2   To ensure that the delivery of training meets individual needs and is in their best interests, training organisations should provide purchasers of the training with information on policy development, health and safety information and advise them about relevant and up to date sector guidance. This should include information on how to involve individuals who use their service in developing their own behaviour support plan.

2.3.3   Training organisations must ensure that training is delivered in the context of the following principles:

- people's human rights are protected and upheld at all times

- person centred approaches that seek to identify and enhance the individual's quality of life

- all individuals must be treated with compassion, dignity and kindness

- services should take all possible and reasonable steps to keep people safe and free from harm

2.3.4   Training must specifically emphasise that any restrictive physical interventions:

- must only be considered when all other available and appropriate methods of primary and secondary prevention and non-physical reactive intervention have been tried, reviewed and evaluated to be ineffective

- must be accompanied by the consent of the individual or a best interest decision and considered within the appropriate legislative context

- must only be used as a last resort being consistent with managing behaviours that challenge and the risk presented

- must employ the minimum reasonable amount of force

- must be used for the shortest possible time

- must be followed by a debrief for all of those involved, which is appropriate to their needs and individual requirements

- should be underpinned by individual behaviour assessment and support plans and should include a restrictive physical intervention reduction plan. The individual behaviour support plan should be reviewed following any incident that results in the use of a restrictive physical intervention. All of the plans should be reviewed every six months as a minimum

- should be followed by a debrief of the incident when this involves the use of an unplanned response or emergency intervention. If appropriate a full behaviour assessment should be undertaken and/or a new or reviewed support plan developed.

2.4 Risk assessment, health and safety and training delivery

2.4.1   Training must take place in a safe and suitable environment. There must be sufficient space to avoid danger from obstacles such as furniture and fittings. When participants are required to kneel, sit or lie on the floor, the surface should be covered with a suitable gym mat or equivalent covering to provide greater comfort and protection from possible injuries.

2.4.2   Training organisations should ensure that a course registration document is developed. This document should record:

- the date and venue of training

- the names of the participants, including their designation and place of work

- the signature of each participant to a statement declaring their 'fitness to participate', both at the start and on completion of the course which confirms that they:

  - are currently physically fit to participate

  - are responsible for reporting any reason why they are unable to continue to train during the training session

  - are responsible for reporting any injuries that they may incur during training

2.4.3   Training organisations may wish to guide
         participants through gentle mobilisation
         activities to ensure that they have 'warmed up'
         prior to any instruction in physical skills. This
         is at the discretion of the training organisations
         and should be within the abilities of the course
         participants. Where mobilisation activities are
         used, the training organisation should ensure
         that they have been risk assessed, using the
         criteria set out at 2.4.10 and 2.4.11, as safe
         and 'fit for purpose' for participants. In addition,
         training organisations should provide to their
         purchasers a detailed safety case for using
         such activities that identifies how and why their
         use will decrease the risk of subsequent injury
         to participants during training.

2.4.4   BILD recommends that the ratio of trainers to
         participants should be 1:10. As a minimum,
         all training must be delivered at a ratio of
         1:15 (trainer to participants) and a cohort
         of participants must not exceed 30.

2.4.5   In exceptional circumstances, where it is
         necessary to train a group of more than 30
         people, an accredited training organisation
         must inform the BILD Accreditation Scheme
         in writing, and provide evidence of the written
         agreement covering the above criteria.
         BILD will then issue a 'notice of exceptional
         circumstances for delivery of accredited
         training'. The number of trainers must be

consistent with criteria 2.4.4 above, regardless of the numbers of participants. In these circumstances, training organisations and purchasers must also ensure that the length of the course is adequate and that the content is consistent with the standards of the *Code of Practice*. Where this is necessary, there must be a written agreement between the training and purchasing organisations that sets out:

- the reasons for working with a larger group

- any limitations that this will impose on the training programme

- any additional concerns regarding health and safety during the training and how any identified risks will be overcome

- an agreement on what limitations training a larger group will have in assessing and achieving the agreed learning outcomes

- the details of any training that is required to ensure the appropriate levels of competence among course participants with the possibility of more frequent refresher training

2.4.6   All training organisations and their accredited trainers must be covered by professional indemnity and public liability insurance. Copies of current certificates of insurance should be made available to purchasing organisations.

2.4.7   Training organisations should satisfy them-selves that consultants for their organisation working under a franchise agreement or as self employed trainers, can demonstrate that they have the appropriate insurance for the activities they undertake.

2.4.8   Organisations that deliver training on their own premises should ensure that staff members, who are suitably trained in first aid are available when training in physical skills is delivered.

2.4.9   Training organisations should provide the information to purchasing organisations that BILD recommends that refresher training should take place annually (within 12 months of initial training) to ensure that their training remains valid as an accredited curriculum.

2.4.10   Training organisations must ensure that they have evaluated the foreseeable risks associated with all of the physical techniques included within their curriculum. All physical techniques taught by the training organisation must be risk assessed by an independent individual or organisation that can demonstrate appropriate expertise in each of the following areas:

- professional assessment of risk

- manual handling and health and safety legislation

- biomechanics and physiology
  (relevant to child and adult anatomy)

- psychological assessment

2.4.11   The risk assessment should record:

- the suitability of the techniques for various
  populations including for use with adults,
  children and young people and identify
  any differential risks

- the psychological impact of any techniques

- any potential risk of harm to staff members
  using the techniques

- any potential risk of harm to health or any
  safety implications for the individuals using
  the service

- that the identified physical techniques never
  impede breathing

- evidence that the techniques being taught
  do not intentionally inflict pain and are
  not developed with pain compliance as
  a means of control. BILD is morally and
  ethically opposed to the use of deliberate
  infliction of pain as a means of control
  in the sectors of care and education
  covered by this guidance

- evidence that the techniques taught
  avoid vulnerable parts of the body
  (eg neck, chest and sexual areas)

- evidence that the techniques avoid hyperextension and hyperflexion of limbs and joints

- evidence that the techniques do not employ potentially dangerous positions, including positions that may compromise the breathing or the welfare and safety of the person based upon their individual characteristics and profile which must be considered in the context of all relevant individual risk assessments

- that the techniques do not conflict with any relevant official guidance (for example the Welsh Government prohibition of the use of prone restraint)

- clear guidance on the characteristic of each technique, how it is to be taught and the importance of individuals using each technique as taught and not attempting unsupervised modifications

2.4.12   The risk assessment of the physical skills taught in training should be subject to independent review every three years, or sooner if the techniques change or are modified by the training organisation.

2.4.13   It is acknowledged through research that techniques that impact on airways, breathing and circulation carry significantly increased risks. Such techniques should be avoided

---

wherever possible. Their inclusion as part of a taught curriculum should be reviewed by the training organisation annually. Training organisations should have a clear written rationale for their continued inclusion within any taught programme. The rationale for inclusion in any adult setting should take account of the DH guidance for England, sections 70, 71 and 72 (Department of Health, 2014).

2.4.14   At least annually, training organisations should review the data associated with incidents of injury, accident or other incidents that arise during the delivery of their training. The training organisation must be able to demonstrate that this data is contributing to their internal review of the risks associated with physical skills and the impact on their teaching.

2.4.15   It is accepted that discomfort may be an unwanted side effect of physical intervention. However, any techniques that deliberately cause pain, or that rely on the use of pain in order to be effective, or which have been developed with the intention of causing pain, or that use deliberate hyperflexion, (eg where an individual is bent forward in the seated position), are not supported by this *Code of Practice*. Any curriculum that knowingly includes such techniques will not be accredited by BILD.

2.5　Training course organisation and curriculum development

2.5.1　Training organisations are expected to design training based on the needs indicated by the behaviour audit, training needs analysis and risk assessment. It is the responsibility of the purchasing organisation to undertake these, but the training organisation may need to offer support in undertaking the audit and assessment or in providing a template for the collection of the relevant information. This information should be available at least one month prior to the delivery of training.

2.5.2　The training programme and curriculum development must include opportunities for participants to explore their attitudes, values and beliefs and to reflect on their own practice.

2.5.3　The training must also address any issues relating to the gender, culture and diversity of the course participants and the individuals who are being supported.

Children and young people

2.5.4　Training for services that educate, care for and support children and young people must be specific to the needs of these groups. The curriculum design must take account of developmental models, identifying and addressing the specific needs and circumstances of children and young people who might experience a range of developmental disabilities. These include intellectual disability, autism, attachment difficulties or educational and/or social vulnerability. This *Code of Practice* can be applied across all services and settings for children and young people including mainstream schools, special education settings, residential schools and colleges, children who are looked after, families and foster carers.

2.5.5   In school settings, it is advisable that the training is delivered in the context of the specific environment and includes preventative classroom management techniques. This should emphasise that restrictive physical interventions should be used as a last resort being reasonable, appropriate, proportionate and necessary, refer to section 2.3.4.

2.5.6   Physical skills taught within settings for children and young people must take account of their specific age, developmental level, size and the risk to them and others.

2.5.7   In all circumstances, training providers must ensure that a clear written rationale exists for any training that is delivered. Commissioned training must place an emphasis on child centred approaches that are individualised and aimed at reducing the intensity, frequency and impact of a child's or young person's behaviour whilst reducing the risk to them and others.

2.5.8   Any training organisation that teaches restrictive intervention techniques, which research demonstrates have additional and significant risks in services for children and young people, must provide written evidence that shows why the technique(s) has been selected for an individual child or young person. This includes any restrictive physical interventions on the floor. Such techniques should only be taught within an appropriate context and address the needs of the individual, the service and the staff who support or educate them. The trainer should ensure that the purchasing organisation can provide evidence that:

- the named child or young person has had a full assessment of their target behaviour and that a positive behaviour support plan has been developed for and with them

- there is an up to date risk assessment for the child or young person related to the target behaviour

- a restrictive physical intervention reduction plan has been developed and will be implemented in line with specific review dates and plans. This may be included in the behaviour support plan, positive handling plan or risk assessment

- there is a record of everyone who has been trained in these techniques which include the date when the skills were taught and the specific techniques that each person has been found competent to use. The training must be specifically reviewed and refreshed as regularly as is required for the purchasing organisation to comply with health and safety legislation. BILD recommends this takes place at least every 12 months

Adult services

2.5.9   The development of curricula for training in services that educate, care for and support adults must be specific to the needs of adults. The curriculum design must take account of the needs of the adult population who are being supported by the purchasing organisation, including information on the specific support needs of individuals (eg those with severe learning disability or autistic spectrum conditions).

2.5.10   All training must place an emphasis on person centred approaches, individual support planning and proactive support.

2.5.11   Restrictive physical interventions that involve holding an individual on the floor must only be taught with reference to use with a named individual and the team who supports them. The training organisation and purchasing organisation must demonstrate that:

- a full behavioural assessment has been undertaken

- a current behaviour risk assessment is in place

- a restrictive physical intervention reduction plan is in place

- a record is kept of everyone trained in the use of high risk techniques along with the date when the skills were taught and the particular techniques each person has been found competent to use. Training must be regularly reviewed and refreshed as regularly as is required for the purchasing organisation to comply with health and safety legislation. BILD recommends that this takes place at least every 12 months

2.5.12   Some services present higher risks to staff working within them, to the individuals using the service and others including visitors and family members. These may include, but are not limited to, forensic services, some assessment and treatment services and services for people who are detained by the Home Office at the order of the courts. Equally a service that does not provide the necessary organisational responses in terms of resources even where the individuals do not present with significant behavioural challenges could constitute a high risk service. In such settings, the risks may be higher than in other services and therefore there may be a requirement for training organisations to include a broader curriculum of physical skills. However, any such broader curriculum must not contravene criteria 2.4.15 of this *Code of Practice*. As in all other situations, the training should be based on a behaviour audit and take into account the local risk assessment. In these settings, it is important that the training reflects the significant needs of the individuals who are being educated, cared for and supported.

2.5.13   The training should place an emphasis on person centred approaches that are individualised and aimed at reducing the intensity, frequency and impact of a person's behaviour whilst reducing the risk to them and others. It must take account of the risks presented to team members, which at times may be substantial and difficult to predict. This may be due to the severity of the challenging behaviour and the need to manage it in the short term before there have been opportunities to devise and fully implement any proactive strategies.

2.5.14　As a minimum, training organisations must ensure that the core theoretical content of any training covers the following:

- populations

- definitions

- proactive and positive support of behaviour

- respecting all individuals – rights and best interests

- de-escalation and reactive behaviour management strategies

- legislation and guidance relating to restrictive physical interventions

- promoting the safe and appropriate use of restrictive physical interventions

- post incident management and debrief

Training organisations should consider how they can develop and/or deliver training in partnership with individuals who have a lived experience of services and their family carers.

The details below are provided as reference for training organisations to consider in relation to course content.

Populations

An understanding of the characteristics of the population of individuals that are supported including issues relating to gender, culture and diversity.

Courses may include:

- developmental levels
- identified and diagnosed conditions
- individual communication methods, needs and preferences
- age
- vulnerability factors and personal history including any experience of abuse, chaotic placement history or traumatic life events
- individual physical characteristics including size
- physical and medical conditions
- opportunities to explore an understanding of the experiences of individuals who use a service and of their family members

Training content must be relevant to and provide an overview of the issues relevant to the service provision of the purchasing organisation including:

- adults and children with a learning disability
- adults and children with autistic spectrum conditions
- pupils with special educational needs
- children with social, emotional and behavioural difficulties associated with behaviours that challenge
- adults with a learning disability and or autism who are detained under the appropriate mental health legislation, children and young people (up to the age of 19) who are detained in semi-secure and secure settings or who are detained under the relevant mental health legislation
- families and family carers, including foster carers and those offering short breaks and support to children, young people and adults with learning disabilities, autism and social, emotional and behavioural difficulties

Definitions

The training should provide information about relevant definitions taken from national guidance and/or local policy. As a minimum, this should include the following terms:

- challenging behaviour
- positive behaviour support
- primary, secondary and reactive strategies
- restrictive practices
- restrictive physical interventions
- time out and seclusion

The training must reference the origins of any definitions used identifying whether they are from national or local policies and guidance, published literature or other resources.

Proactive and positive support of behaviour

The training should provide:

- information on common contributing biological factors in the development of behaviour that challenges services
- information on the common contributing non-biological and environmental factors in the development of behaviour that challenges services
- an understanding of the functions of behaviour
- an overview of functional assessment and how to implement proactive support in the context of behaviour support planning
- the importance of developing individual behaviour support plans for people who use services that describe the agreed methods of intervention for the proactive support of behaviour and the primary and secondary prevention strategies
- the importance of proactive behavioural risk assessment

Respecting all individuals – rights and best interests

The training must include information about:

- an individual's right to be consulted about their care and treatment including the strategies and interventions that affects them. This must include the protection of dignity, human rights and the fundamental freedoms of individuals

- understanding the views and opinions of individuals who are subject to behavioural interventions and/or restrictive physical interventions and how this may impact on the relationships built between staff and the individuals who use services

- the relevance of age, age related and developmental issues that may be particularly important in services for individuals with learning disabilities and autism

- an understanding of the relevance of gender, culture and diversity issues that may affect the use of physical contact of all types, and the need to avoid inappropriate physical contact both in training and practice

- the process of best interest decision making, with reference to the relevant legislation and guidance for the country the purchasing organisation works in

De-escalation and reactive behaviour management strategies

The training should include:

- information on conflict resolution and de-escalation strategies that may prevent any requirement for restrictive physical intervention
- information on how to reduce the risks to any individual during a crisis situation, including space, posture, body language and communication
- information about specific physical skills for the safe breakaway and disengagement from physical contact to protect personal safety
- details of appropriate interventions where the behavioural audit and risk assessment identifies a need for restrictive physical interventions

Legislation and guidance relating to restrictive physical interventions

There must also be an overview of the relevant legislation and any statutory and non-statutory guidance for adults or children and young people. The legislation and guidance covered should be tailored to meet the needs of the population supported by the participants, including children's or adult services, learning disability and/or autism and/or mental health and the context of any behaviour that challenges.

The overview of legislation, guidance and policy will be relevant to the jurisdiction of the purchasing organisation or specific service.

Promoting the safe and appropriate use of restrictive physical interventions

The training provided might include information about:

- the assessment of any health conditions that would place an individual at risk in the event of a specific physical intervention being used

- the common physical and psychological contra-indications for the use of physical interventions

- the difference between 'escorting',' touching' and 'holding', referring to the manner of intervention, degree of force and motivation

- the use of gradients of control and the principles of minimum force and minimum duration

- the avoidance of potentially dangerous postures and positioning, with reference to ergonomic, physiological and biomechanical factors

- potential contributory factors in restraint related injuries and deaths including positional asphyxia, excited delirium, substance misuse and pharmacological issues

- the evidence base of increased risks associated with floor restraints and the additional safeguards required for these techniques of restrictive physical intervention:

  o floor holds (prone or supine) should be avoided (as far as is practicably possible) and must not arise from the direct and intentional action by staff to forcibly control an individual on the floor as a means of coercion

  o physical interventions must not involve the deliberate application of pain by staff, or as a result of the use of holds whereby movement by an individual will in itself induce pain

  o individuals must not be restrained in a way that impacts on their airway, breathing or circulation

  o there should be no deliberate use of techniques whereby a person is allowed to fall, unsupported, to the floor

  o for adults services in England this must make reference to the DH guidance, sections 70–72 (Department of Health, 2014)

- the monitoring of an individual's physical wellbeing whilst physical interventions are employed
- the need for a clear and effective procedure for recognising when a restrictive physical intervention must be stopped and when an emergency first aid intervention is required due to serious injury or threat to life
- physical care, including how to summon help and the appropriate course of action in the event of any accidental injury in the workplace whilst physical interventions are being used
- procedures for the assessment of an individual following the use of a physical intervention
- the importance of ensuring good quality and clear behaviour support plans document any restrictive physical interventions as a structured approach and response to any identified specific behaviours
- the importance of restraint reduction and how to achieve this as an outcome

Post incident management and debrief

The training should include information about:

- the importance of accurate recording, reporting, reviewing and monitoring of the occurrence of behaviours that challenge and the use of restrictive physical interventions
- the importance of an appropriate, evidence based system of debrief that provides emotional and psycho-logical support for individuals and staff following any incidents and/or the use of physical interventions
- the importance of reviewing support plans and reactive management following incidents and on a regular and ongoing basis
- the need to keep the key people in the person's life informed about the individual's behaviour support, identifying ongoing learning for the organisation involved

2.5.15   It is imperative that all training in the use of restrictive physical interventions is specifically targeted to enable staff to better support individual needs and individual situations. Training a range of physical skills for all participants on a course is not acceptable and is not supported by this *Code of Practice*. Training must be delivered to services with a clear focus on individual behaviour support plans and individual strategies.

2.5.16   In consultation with the purchasing organisation, the training organisation should specify in writing the content of the training curriculum and list all of the restrictive physical intervention techniques that will be taught.

2.5.17   Training organisations should document the training aims and objectives and intended learning outcomes in lesson plans appropriate to each section of the course curriculum delivered.

2.5.18   The lesson plans should include the indicative length of time to be spent on each section of the full curriculum delivered.

2.5.19   Training organisations must provide appropriate assessment criteria to establish whether the intended learning outcomes have been achieved during the delivery of a course.

2.6 Reporting, recording and record keeping of training

2.6.1 Training organisations are responsible for ensuring that their trainers maintain complete, accurate and up to date records of each course they deliver. Records should be maintained and retained by the training organisations for a period of time that is consistent with legislative requirements. Each record should cover:

- the title of the course, duration and details of the trainers involved

- the learning aims and objectives, content and outcomes

- the details of which breakaway, personal safety and restrictive physical interventions were taught

- details of the organisation purchasing the training

- the name of each course participant, including their employing organisation and the setting or service where they work

- a signature confirming the fitness to participate of each participant

- a record of health issues and physical status disclosed by any participant that might compromise their ability to participate in training

- theory test scores for each participant

- written feedback on the competent application of physical skills demonstrated by each participant

- details of all of the participants which identifies who satisfactorily completed the course and demonstrated competence and who did not

- any action taken in respect of participants who failed to demonstrate competence

- details of any injuries or accidents reportable under health and safety legislation occurring during the training, in compliance with Health and Safety Executive *Reporting of Injuries, Diseases and Dangerous Occurrences Regulations* (RIDDOR)

- details of all incidents in which the usual safety guidelines were breached

- arrangements for follow up support, with particular reference to any participant who failed to meet the competency criteria

- arrangements for refresher training and the date on which it will occur for all purchasing organisations and details of the members of the original course who attended refresher training

- participant evaluation of the course, including comments on whether the course fulfilled its stated aims and met their training needs. Any concerns about the conduct or values of trainers or fellow participants should be retained

2.6.2 Training organisations must ensure that their recording systems comply with the Data Protection Act 1998. The Data Protection Act 1998 requires businesses to give details about the way they process personal information to the Information Commissioner's Office (ICO) for inclusion in a public register, unless they are exempt. All training organisations must hold an up to date certificate of compliance.

2.7 Monitoring performance and the evaluation of participants

2.7.1 The knowledge and performance of each participant should be evaluated and recorded in respect of every part of the course. Areas to be included are:

- attitudes as reflected in the language and behaviour used during the course

- knowledge of appropriate theoretical concepts, approaches and strategies

- knowledge of the principles underpinning the safe use of restrictive physical interventions

- knowledge relating to the ethical and legal aspects in implementing the use of restrictive physical interventions

- competence in each practical technique taught

2.7.2   Training organisations should establish assessment criteria that are consistent with the level of the training that is being provided. The criteria should distinguish between introductory level training, refresher training courses and accredited trainer courses.

2.7.3   Training organisations delivering training at accredited trainer or train the trainer level must demonstrate that the theory test examines the participants' understanding of the course content and the requirements of adult learning, including an understanding of different learning styles and teaching methods. In addition, all train the trainer level training must require participants to demonstrate practical skills in theory and physical skill teaching as part of the assessment of competence.

2.7.4   At all levels of training, a test of knowledge should be included with the scores being recorded and evaluated as one aspect of demonstrating that the learning outcomes have been achieved.

2.7.5   Each training organisation should establish assessment criteria and a rationale for every practical technique taught within its courses. The criteria should include:

- the application of the technique

- an understanding of the relevant safety principles and issues relating to risk

- the gradient approach to restrictive physical interventions

2.7.6   All participants should be given verbal feed-back about their performance, as a minimum. Participants who do not reach the required standard of the course must be referred to the purchasing organisation and given advice and support on how they can meet the assessment criteria. They should be encouraged to retake the training at a future date if possible.

2.7.7   The training organisation should provide purchasing organisations with written feedback on the assessed performance of each course participant. Written feedback should be provided to any participants who fail to reach the required standard and to their managers. This should include:

- the identified areas in which they have failed to provide evidence of competence

- the actions that can be taken to enable them to achieve competence in these areas

- the implications of their current level of competence when working with individuals who present challenging behaviour

2.7.8   If a failure to provide evidence of competence has implications for the person's future employment or job role then this must be managed by the purchasing organisation and is not the responsibility of the training organisation.

2.7.9   Training organisations must provide appropriate channels for any participant or purchasing organisation to raise concerns, or complaints associated with training that they have received.

2.7.10   Training organisations must make purchasing organisations aware that they are responsible for maintaining the skills of their staff at an appropriate and safe level, under health and safety legislation. Training organisations must make purchasing organisations aware that BILD recommends that all levels of training are refreshed at least annually in order to support:

- the retention of an appropriate knowledge base in proactive support of behaviour

- reviewing and refreshing the safe application of physical skills techniques that may still be required as part of the duties of staff

- the review of current practice within the specific work setting

2.8   Support to trainers

2.8.1   Training organisations with accredited trainers working under their auspices (as employees, consultants or under a franchise or license agreement), have additional responsibilities to ensure the continuing competence of their trainers and in maintaining the required records. The training organisations must:

- maintain a current record of accredited and in-house trainers permitted to use the organisation's name or deliver the model of training promoted by the organisation

- ensure this record matches with the information available on the BILD website, including the accredited trainer names and ID numbers and the provision of accurate information about the courses they are able to deliver as accredited trainers

- require accredited trainers to maintain a record of the information set out at section 2.6.1 of this *Code of Practice* for each course that they deliver

- carry out regular and systematic audits of all training records, including those of its accredited trainers, to ensure that they comply with the evaluation and record keeping requirements of this *Code of Practice* and other relevant legislation and local policy

- at least annually ensure that all accredited trainers update and review their skills, knowledge and competence to teach

- maintain records of the continuous professional development (CPD) of all accredited trainers

- provide continuous professional development opportunities for their accredited trainers in any relevant fields associated with the training that they deliver

- maintain a record of any disciplinary action taken by the organisation in relation to their current trainers or those employed in the preceding five-year period

2.8.2   In order to support accredited and in-house trainers to maintain an adherence to this *Code of Practice* training organisations must take the appropriate steps to support them to understand their responsibilities and offer further information for clarification where necessary.

2.8.3   Training organisations should ensure a procedure is in place to carry out the assessment of potential course participants for train the trainer courses who will subsequently deliver in-house training on their behalf for a purchasing organisation. They must be satisfied that any potential course participant nominated by a purchasing organisation for train the trainer courses has:

- appropriate professional and practice expertise

- knowledge of positive behaviour support approaches and proactive strategies for managing behaviour that challenges

- the knowledge, adaptability and personal qualities required to deliver adult learning

Training organisations should support purchasing organisations by providing information on the expectations of the role of the in-house trainer and the requirements of adherence to this *Code of Practice* alongside any details about their assessment of potential participants.

2.8.4   All training organisations must ensure that they provide regular opportunities for their accredited and in-house trainers to update their knowledge and skills. Wherever possible, this should be extended to all of the trainers employed in purchasing organisations that deliver in-house training. The expectation is that all trainers can provide evidence of formal development opportunities (over and above practising physical skills) relating to their delivery of training in the subject of behaviour support for a minimum of eight hours annually.

2.8.5   The training organisations must provide each trainer with a trainer agreement. This document should provide information on the trainer's accredited status or certification to deliver a specific course. For accredited trainers the agreement may also incorporate general terms and conditions of employment as an accredited trainer with an accredited organisation and reference the specific criteria of this *Code of Practice.*

2.8.6   The training agreements for individuals who have attended train the trainer courses must set out the conditions of their certification including information on what happens should an in-house trainer change jobs and move to another purchasing organisation.

2.8.7   The trainer agreement should also provide information on:

- the training organisation's approach to addressing complaints, concerns and compliments

- the trainer's requirements in relation to adherence to this *Code of Practice*

- how trainers can access support, advice and continuous professional development

- the training organisation's approach to internal quality assurance

2.8.8   Training organisations must:

- offer opportunities for accredited and in-house trainers to develop and maintain their physical skills through regular practice opportunities with other trained staff

- offer opportunities for all trainers to keep up to date with research, evidence and good practice

- ensure all trainers are provided with the time to prepare and deliver training in line with the standards set out in this *Code of Practice*

- ensure trainers have access to the equipment and resources necessary to deliver training

- ensure all training takes place in suitable environments

- ensure that all trainers maintain and update their skills and that this is reviewed on an annual basis

- keep a record of all of the training delivered on behalf of their organisation

Individual trainers

Individual accredited and in-house trainers have a responsibility to ensure that the training they deliver takes account of the following:

3.1 Guidance for all trainers: accredited and in-house

3.1.1　All of the criteria in this section apply to accredited trainers employed by or working for a training organisation that is accredited or is making an application to be accredited within the BILD Accreditation Scheme. Good practice requires in-house trainers who are delivering training within a purchasing organisation, adhere to the standards for accredited trainers, whenever practically possible. All trainers should expect their training organisation to provide them with the required advice and support to implement accurate record keeping, monitoring and evaluation procedures.

3.1.2   When delivering a BILD accredited course, all trainers must ensure that they deliver the training in accordance with this *Code of Practice*.

3.1.3   All trainers must have the opportunity to formally review and update their knowledge and to practise the physical skills that they teach through formal refresher training courses at least every 12 months.

3.1.4   All trainers should undertake a risk assessment of the training environment to satisfy themselves that the space is free from hazards, provides enough room to move around safely and is suitable and conducive to successful training delivery.

3.1.5   At the beginning of every day of course delivery trainers should introduce themselves, outline the expected ground rules and take participants through local 'house-keeping' information.

3.1.6   During training trainers have a responsibility to make participants aware that the trainer has a duty to report any concerns that arise to their employing organisation. This may include:

- inappropriate comments, values or beliefs expressed by any participant

- observed inappropriate sexual behaviour, such as inappropriate physical contact or comments

- information shared in the training about the mistreatment of individuals using the services

- information shared about inappropriate approaches including abusive interventions

- negative and discriminatory language or actions

- poor performance in terms of the skills, knowledge or attitudes required for the safe use of restrictive physical interventions

3.1.7 Trainers must inform participants that they too have the same duty to report any concerns during the course of their employment. If any of the above concerns arise then they must inform their manager and follow the policies and procedures of their employing organisation. This must be clearly stated at the start of the training course and supported by written statements within the course materials.

3.1.8 If a trainer has any concerns about the conduct of a participant and/or their expressed opinions during the training, this should initially be discussed with the participant. Where the trainer has continuing concerns, these must be reported to a manager within the participant's purchasing or employing organisation. In all such instances, the trainer should keep a written record of what happened and their actions in response.

3.1.9   During the training, trainers should remind participants of the risk assessment procedures of their employing organisation and their personal responsibilities in relation to:

- guarding against the risk of injury during the training and immediately reporting any subsequent injury to the trainers

- reporting any existing injuries and disabilities that may pose health and safety risks to their own safety and welfare and those of other participants during training

- reporting all injuries or adverse events in accordance with statutory guidance, eg Health and Safety Executive, *Reporting of Injuries, Diseases and Dangerous Occurrences Regulations* (RIDDOR) to the purchasing organisation, including any sustained during the training

3.1.10   The trainer has the right to exclude from the course anyone that they believe to be unsuitable for training on the following grounds:

- their health and/or physical status/ presentation on the course

- their attitudes, values and beliefs as displayed on the course

- their behaviour towards the trainer and/or other participants

- their time keeping and attendance throughout the course

3.1.11   Any such exclusion should be subsequently confirmed in writing to the purchasing organisation or the participant's manager if it is an in-house course. The employing organisation retains the responsibility for the health and safety of employees prior to and throughout the training course.

3.1.12   All trainers must ensure that suitable first aid facilities and equipment are readily accessible at the training venue.Trainers should have the means and ability to summon emergency services to the venue should a serious injury occur during a training session.

3.1.13   All trainers are expected to maintain professional records and a record of continuing professional practice. For many professionals this is a requirement of their everyday practice and their ongoing professional registration.

3.1.14   All trainers should ensure that they are specifically insured to teach physical skills.

3.2   **BILD accredited trainers**

3.2.1   The term 'accredited trainer' refers to trainers directly paid by an accredited organisation to deliver an accredited course on their behalf. At the point of accreditation and at subsequent regular intervals, each organisation that is accredited under the BILD Accreditation Scheme will be required to provide details of each trainer that they wish to be accredited.

3.2.2   All accredited trainers will have an individual accreditation ID card issued by BILD. This will include a Unique Accredited Trainer Reference (UATR) and a photograph of the trainer. This ID card must be visible and available throughout training delivery.

3.2.3   Accredited trainers employed within training organisations that are adhering to the *Code of Practice* must have a professional or vocational qualification that may include:

- a qualification for working within health and social care

- a Diploma in Social Work

- a teaching or education-based qualification

- a health professional registration such as nurse or occupational therapist

3.2.4   Accredited trainers employed by training organisations must be able to evidence having been employed in an environment that supports people with learning disabilities or autistic spectrum conditions or special educational needs or severe behavioural, emotional or social difficulties, for a period of no less than two years.

3.2.5   All accredited trainers must also hold or be
         working towards a coaching or teaching
         qualification that qualifies them to teach
         adult learners.

3.2.6   Accredited trainers must be able to demonstrate
         that they periodically review their ability to
         deliver training that addresses:

         ● primary and secondary prevention strategies

         ● reactive strategies

         ● risk assessment

         ● individual behaviour assessment and
           support plans

         ● legislative frameworks and national
           guidance

3.2.7   Accredited trainers should demonstrate a clear
         understanding that any training in the use of
         restrictive physical interventions is delivered in
         an appropriate context of positive behaviour
         support and functional assessment with
         reference to the needs of the people who use
         the services of the purchasing organisation.

3.2.8   Accredited trainers delivering training in
         restrictive physical interventions should
         hold an appropriate and up to date first aid
         qualification. The expectation is that this
         certificate will be for a course lasting at least
         one whole day and cover basic emergency

---

first aid to manage minor injuries. This will enable them to respond to any injuries that might arise during training.

3.2.9   Accredited trainers must be covered by professional indemnity and public liability insurance. Copies of a current certificate of insurance should be available in the training room.

3.2.10   Accredited trainers working as consultants for a training organisation under a franchise agreement or as self employed trainers must ensure that they have the appropriate insurance for the activities that they undertake. Valid insurance documentation should be submitted annually for review to the organisation for which they deliver training.

Glossary

Accredited trainer

A trainer who has received accreditation from the BILD Accreditation Scheme and has a BILD Unique Accredited Trainer Reference (UATR).

Accredited training

An approved programme of learning or training model that has been assessed by the accreditation panel as adhering to the standards in the *BILD Code of Practice*. Training organisations seeking accreditation are required to list all of the programmes or training models for which they are seeking accreditation.

BILD accredited training organisation

An organisation delivering an approved programme of learning or training model that has been assessed by the accreditation panel, as adhering to the standards in the

BILD Code of Practice. The details of such organisations and their portfolio of accredited courses are available to view on the BILD website at www.bild.org.uk/codeofpractice.

Behavioural audit

A process to establish the 'behaviour/s of concern' for an individual, a service or within a group of services. This information is used to prioritise the 'behaviour/s of concern' and inform the planning of primary, secondary and reactive strategies following the functional assessment of the behaviour/s. The behaviour audit and risk assessments inform the required level of reactive physical interventions needed in the short term.

Behaviour support plan

A behaviour support plan provides detailed information relating to all aspects of a person's behaviour and how to support them. The plan is person centred in its approach setting out details about the individual's behaviour including hypotheses about the function/s of a particular behaviour, known antecedents, triggers, risks, settings for the behaviour as well as how the known behaviours should be recorded when they occur. The plan also describes the proactive and reactive strategies that those supporting the individual should follow to improve the person's quality of life and reduce risky behaviours.

BILD Accreditation Scheme

The process of assessment by an accreditation panel of adherence to the *BILD Code of Practice.* This is a voluntary scheme.

Debrief

A reflective process that explores what happened before, during and after an incident. The intention is to carry out an analysis and evaluation to inform how similar incidents may be avoided or better managed in the future. Debrief involves the individual concerned with the incident and those who were present and involved with any intervention or support. Different types of debriefing may be used by organisations to collect information, help the individuals they support and for the support and supervision of their staff.

Individual who uses a service

A child, young person or adult supported in a health, social care or educational setting.

In-house trainer

An employee of an organisation who has attended and successfully completed an accredited train the trainer course, provided by an accredited training organisation.

In-house training

Training delivered to a group of employees from the same organisation and delivered by a trainer who is also an employee of the organisation. The trainer will have attended a BILD accredited train the trainer course and be certified by the accredited training organisation to deliver one of their accredited courses.

Participant

A person attending a training course.

Positive behaviour support (PBS)

The BILD *International Journal of Positive Behavioural Support* (Gore et al, 2013) has defined positive behavioural support as a framework:

- that enhances the quality of life for the individual and others involved in their life

- for developing an understanding of the challenging behaviour displayed by an individual, based on an assessment of their social and physical environment and the broader context within which it occurs

- that is developed with the full inclusion and involvement of the individual (child, young person or adult) being supported, their family members and/or their advocate

- to develop, implement and evaluate the effectiveness of a personalised and enduring system of support

PBS is an approach which incorporates the safe use of reactive strategies (possibly including restrictive practices) alongside proactive primary and secondary preventative approaches. Reactive strategies are required to make a situation safe and return a person to a state where they can resume their regular activities and lifestyle. A considerable evidence base has emerged over recent decades that shows the clear benefits of PBS as a strategy in terms of improving the quality of life of individuals who use services and in reducing challenging behaviours.

Positive handling plan

(see behaviour support plan)

Proactive strategies

These are strategies to prevent a person's behaviour presenting a risk to themselves or other people. These should be person centred and focus on improving the quality of life for the individual. Proactive strategies are based on a detailed understanding of the individual's likes and dislikes, dreams, aspirations and support needs. They may include changing aspects of the individual's environment to reduce the likelihood of behaviour that challenges occurring.

Purchasing organisation

An organisation seeking to purchase training in behaviour support including restrictive physical interventions to equip their employees with the necessary values, skills and knowledge to provide good care, support or education. Purchasing organisations support individuals whose behaviour may be described as challenging in health, social care or educational settings.

Reactive strategies

These are strategies used in response to situations of risk. They involve managing a challenging situation in order to minimise the immediate risk. These strategies are person centred and are used to manage an immediate risk and keep everyone safe. They do not aim to deliver long term and lasting behavioural change.

Restrictive physical interventions

The implementation of any practice or practices that restrict an individual's movement, liberty and freedom to act independently without coercion or consequence. Restrictive practices are highly coercive actions that are deliberately enacted to prevent a person from pursuing a particular course of action.

Restrictive physical interventions reduction plan

This is usually part of a positive handling plan or behaviour support plan. It aims to reduce the use of restrictive practices, including restrictive physical interventions.

Restrictive practices

'Interventions aimed at reactively managing behaviour that challenges, as a last resort. They are not aimed at changing the behaviour itself but at simply managing the associated risk'. (Paley-Wakefield, 2013).

Restrictive practices may take the form of:

- physical intervention
- seclusion
- environmental restraint
- mechanical restraint
- chemical restraint
- Pro Re Nata (PRN) medication
- rapid tranquilisation
- long term segregation

Risk assessment

The identification and evaluation of the severity of risks dependent upon specific decisions and actions. This judgement is then balanced against an assessment of the likelihood of these risks happening. This process must guard against the negative effects of being too cautious, which can lead to a reluctance to pursue positive risk taking. It is important to ensure that:

- procedures for risk assessment are positive and helpful to all involved

- activities or environments that are associated with risk are identified

- the likelihood of any adverse outcomes for the individual are identified

- the consequences of any potential outcomes are fully considered and active plans are agreed in response to each eventuality

- all relevant information is recorded

- regular reviews are undertaken

Train the trainer courses

Courses designed to develop the values, skills and knowledge required to deliver accredited programmes of learning or training models to participants who will go on to provide in-house training. Such courses develop the participants' ability to train others in addition to ensuring their understanding of the course content.

Trainer agreement

Sometimes referred to as a contract this is a document that sets out the responsibilities of an individual trainer in relation to both the *BILD Code of Practice* and their general employment terms and conditions.

Training needs analysis

A process undertaken in partnership between the purchasing organisation and the training organisation by which the content of the training to be delivered is decided. This will involve understanding the current behaviour/s of concern, risks and other issues that are being managed by the service or group of services being trained. It will assess the current knowledge and skills of the participants. Specific physical skills to be taught will be determined from the training needs analysis.

Training organisation

An organisation that delivers a programme of learning or training model including restraint reduction and the use of physical skills. In some circumstances, the training organisation may be a department or section of a purchasing organisation.

Unplanned interventions

Unplanned interventions are aimed at immediate risk management for previously unseen or known behaviour. Such strategies are one off events and their legitimacy is sought with regard to common law.

References and resources

Allen, D (ed) (2002) *Ethical Approaches to Physical Interventions Volume I: Responding to challenging behaviour in people with intellectual disabilities.* Birmingham: BILD Publications

Allen, D (ed) (2009) *Ethical Approaches to Physical Interventions Volume II: Changing the agenda.* Birmingham: BILD Publications

Allen, D (2011) *Reducing the Use of Restrictive Practices with People who have Intellectual Disabilities. A Practical Approach.* Birmingham: BILD

Allen, D and Baker, P (2012) Use of positive behaviour support to tackle challenging behaviour. *Learning Disability Practice*, 15, 1, 18–20

Barcham, L (2011) *Personal Development for Learning Disability Workers.* Birmingham: Learning Matters/BILD

BBC (2011) *Undercover Care: The Abuse Exposed.* BBC Panorama first shown Tuesday 31 May 2011

BILD (2001) BILD *Code of Practice for Trainers in the Use of Physical Interventions.* Birmingham: BILD

BILD (2006) BILD *Code of Practice for the Use of Physical Interventions. A guide for trainers and commissioners of training.* Second edition. Birmingham: BILD

BILD (2010) *BILD Code of Practice for the Use and Reduction of Restrictive Physical Interventions. A guide for trainers and commissioners of training.* Third edition. Birmingham: BILD

Chan, J, French, P and Webber, L (2011) Positive behavioural support and the UNCRPD. *International Journal of Positive Behavioural Support,* 1, 1, 7–13

Cowen, A and Hanson, J (2013) *Partnership Working with Family Carers of People with a Learning Disability and People with Autism.* Birmingham: BILD

Department of Health and Depart-ment for Education and Skills (2002) *Guidance for Restrictive Physical Interventions: How to provide safe services for people with learning disabilities and autistic spectrum disorder.* London: HMSO

Department of Health (2012a) *DH Winterbourne View Review Concordat: Programme of action.* London: DH

Department of Health (2012b) *Transforming Care: A national response to Winterbourne View Hospital. Department of Health review: final report.* London: DH

Department of Health (2014) *Positive and Proactive Care: Reducing the need for restrictive interventions.* London: DH

Equip for Equality (2011) *National Review of Restraint Related Deaths of Children and Adults with Disabilities: The lethal consequences of restraint.* Illinois: Equip for Equality

General Social Care Council (2010) *Codes of Practice for Social Care Workers.* London: General Social Care Council

Gore, N et al (2013) Definition and scope for positive behavioural support. *International Journal of Positive Behavioural Support,* 3, 2, 14–23

Harris, J, Cornick, M, Jefferson, A, Mills, R (2008) *Physical Interventions: A policy framework. Second edition.* Birmingham: BILD Publications

Healthcare Commission and Commission for Social Care Inspection (2006) *Joint Investigation into the Provision of Services for People with Learning Disabilities and Cornwall Partnership NHS Trust.* London: Commission for Healthcare Audit and Inspection

Healthcare Commission (2007) *Investigation into the Services Provided by Sutton and Merton Primary Care Trust.* London: Commission for Healthcare Audit and Inspection

NHS Protect (2013) *Meeting Needs and Reducing Distress. Guidance on the prevention and management of clinically related challenging behaviour in NHS settings.* London: NHS Protect

Paley, S (2012) *Promoting Positive Behaviour when Supporting People with a Learning Disability and People with Autism.* Birmingham: BILD

Paley-Wakefield, S (2012) Is legislation needed to limit the restraint of clients? *Learning Disability Practice*, 15, 2, 24–27

Paley-Wakefield, S (2013) *Framework for Reducing Restrictive Practices.* Birmingham: BILD

Peterson, B, Wilkinson, D, Leadbetter, D, Bradley, P, Bowie, V and Martin A (2011) How corrupted cultures lead to abuse of restraint interventions. *Learning Disability Practice* 14, 7, 24–28

Skills for Care and NDTi (2013) *Supporting Staff Working with People who Challenge Services: Guidance for employers.* Leeds: Skills for Care

Skills for Care and Skills for Health (2013) *National Minimum Training Standards for Healthcare Support Workers and Adult Social Care Workers in England.* Leeds: Skills for Care

Skills for Care and Skills for Health (2013) *Code of Conduct for Healthcare Support Workers and Adult Social Care Workers in England.* Leeds: Skills for Care

Webber, L, Chan, J and French, P (in press) Best practices in Australia in the use of restraint reduction practices for people with intellectual disabilities and autism spectrum disorders. In: Karim, S (ed) *A Human Rights Perspective on Reducing Restrictive Practices in Intellectual Disability and Autistic Spectrum Conditions.* Birmingham: BILD

Section 5: **References and resources**